ISBN-13: 978-1537117669

ISBN-10: 1537117661

Printed in the United States of America.

Contact
collegemhc@gmail.com

Dedicated To

Him

Table of Contents

Introduction

Understanding the meaning of life is the human quest and forms a foundation for psychological well-being.

The purpose of religious and philosophical systems is to provide or explore a comprehensive meaning of life including values and beliefs often taken for granted by individuals within a given society.

A clearer understanding of these values and beliefs, and assisting individuals to engage in this process of clarification, can help to form a foundation for mental health and can be accurately described as Meaning Therapy.

The presentation given here is intended to introduce the values and beliefs given by Jesus of Nazareth, and his earliest followers, who is arguably the most influential Meaning Therapist in human history.

Simply reading this content in its entirety (and related links), will define your positive identity and positive feelings about yourself and others if you choose.

The results include hope for the future, values for healthy living, and support to face challenges and losses common to humanity.

Jesus of Nazareth

"Who do you say I am?"

Legend, Liar, Lunatic, or Lord?

Corroborating witnesses report that Jesus of Nazareth was born of a virgin, changed water to wine, made the blind see, healed the lame, raised the dead, walked on water, calmed the storm, fed 5,000 people with five loaves and two fishes, rose from the dead, and ascended to heaven. According to witnesses and contemporary biographers, this Jesus also made the following claims:

I have always existed. John 8:58; 17:5
I am the First and the Last. Revelation 1:17
I hold the keys to death. Revelation 1:18
I have never sinned. John 8:46
I have all authority on heaven and earth. Matthew 28:18
I and the Father are one. John 10:30
I must be placed above your family. Matthew 10:37
I have authority to forgive sins. Mark 2: 5-12
I am the light of the world. John 8:12
I am prophesied about in the Scriptures. Luke 24:25-27
I am from heaven. John 8:23
I will be resurrected. Mark 8:31
I am the bread of life. John 6:35
I will send the Spirit of God Almighty. John 16:7
I am coming again to the earth. Revelation 22:20
I am a king but not of this world. John 18:37
I came to give life. John 5:24; John 10:10
I am the one through whom you must pray. John 16:23-24
I raise the dead and heal diseases. John 11:38-44; Luke 13:32
I will judge the world on Judgment Day. John 5:22-30
The words I have spoken will condemn at the last day. John 12:47-48
I am the Son of God. Matthew 16:16-17
I will raise the dead at the end of time. John 5:28-29
I am the only way to God. John 14:6
My words will never pass away. Matthew 24:35
If you reject me, you reject God himself. Luke 10:16

-adapted by permission from Douglas A. Jacoby,
Compelling Evidence for God and the Bible *

How To Become A Christian
www.box.com/lovegod

WANTED:

JESUS CHRIST

Alias: The Messiah. The Son Of God. King Of Kings Lord Of Lords. Prince Of Peace. Etc.

- Notorious leader of an underground liberation movement.

- Wanted for the following charges:
  —Practicing medicine, winemaking and food distribution without a license.
  —Interfering with businessmen in the temple.
  —Associating with known criminals, radicals, subversives, prostitutes and street people.
  —Claiming to have the authority to make people into God's children.
  —Tells people to love their enemies, even enemies of the state.

APPEARANCE: Typical hippie type—long hair, beard, robe, sandals.
> Hangs around slum areas, few rich friends, often sneaks out into the desert.

BEWARE: This man is extremely dangerous. His insidiously inflammatory message is particularly dangerous to young people who haven't been taught to ignore him yet. He changes men and claims to set them free.

WARNING: HE IS STILL AT LARGE!

SUBVERSIVE LITERATURE
http://www.box.com/lovegod

Evidences of Jesus the Messiah

*"As to this salvation, the **prophets who prophesied** of the grace that would come to you made careful searches and inquiries, seeking to know what person or time the Spirit of Christ within them was indicating as He predicted the sufferings of Christ and the glories to follow. It was revealed to them that they were not serving themselves, but you, in these things which now have been announced to you through those who preached the gospel to you by the Holy Spirit sent from heaven - things into which angels long to look." - 1 Peter 1:10-12*

The following details from eyewitnesses and their assistants, selected below out of hundreds contained in ancient Hebrew writings that pre-date Jesus, confirm his identity as the Messiah, the promised one who would save Israel as well as the Gentiles who turn to God.

1. **He would be born in the town of Bethlehem.**
- Micah 5:2 (700 BC) fulfilled in Matthew 2:1-6.

Micah 5:2 But you, **Bethlehem** Ephrathah, though you are small among the clans of Judah, out of you will come for me one who will be ruler over Israel, whose origins are from of old, from ancient times.

Matthew 2:1-5 After **Jesus was born in Bethlehem** in Judea, during the time of King Herod, Magi from the east came to Jerusalem and asked, "Where is the one who has been born king of the Jews? We saw his star when it rose and have come to worship him." When King Herod heard this he was disturbed, and all Jerusalem with him. When he had called together all the people's chief priests and teachers of the law, he asked them where the Messiah was to be born. "In Bethlehem in Judea," they replied, "for this is what the prophet has written..."

2. **He would be born of a virgin.**
- Isaiah 7:14 (700 BC) fulfilled in Matthew 1:18-25.

Isaiah 7:14 Therefore the Lord himself will give you a sign: **The virgin will conceive** and give birth to a son, and will **call him Immanuel**.

Matthew 1:18 This is how the birth of Jesus the Messiah came about: His mother Mary was pledged to be married to Joseph, but **before they came together, she was found to be pregnant through the Holy Spirit.**

3. **He would perform miracles.**
– Isaiah 35:5-6 (700 BC) fulfilled in all the gospel accounts.

Isaiah 35:5-6 Then will the eyes of the **blind** be opened and the ears of the **deaf** unstopped. Then will the **lame** leap like a deer, and the **mute tongue** shout for joy.

4. **He would calm the storm.**
- Psalm 107:29 (1000 BC) fulfilled in Mark 4:39.

Psalm 107:29 He **stilled the storm** to a whisper; the waves of the sea were hushed.

Mark 4:39 He got up, rebuked the wind and said to the waves, "Quiet! Be still!" Then the **wind died down and it was completely calm**.

5. **He would speak in parables.**
– Psalm 78:2 (1000 BC) fulfilled in Mark 4:34.

Psalm 78:2 I will open my mouth with a **parable**; I will utter hidden things, things from of old.

Mark 4:34 He did not say anything to them **without using a parable**. But when he was alone with his own disciples, he explained everything.

6. He would enter Jerusalem as a lowly king on a donkey.
– Zechariah 9:9 (500 BC) fulfilled in Matthew 21:6-9.

Zechariah 9:9 Rejoice greatly, Daughter Zion! Shout, Daughter Jerusalem! See, your king comes to you, righteous and victorious, **lowly and riding on a donkey, on a colt, the foal of a donkey**.

Matthew 21:6-8 The disciples went and did as Jesus had instructed them. They **brought the donkey and the colt** and placed their cloaks on them for Jesus to sit on. A very large crowd spread their cloaks on the road, while others cut branches from the trees and spread them on the road.

7. The price of his betrayal would be thirty pieces of silver.
– Zechariah 11:12-13 (500 BC) fulfilled in Matthew 26:14-15 and Matthew 27:3-10.

Zechariah 11:12-13 I told them, "If you think it best, give me my pay; but if not, keep it." So they paid me thirty pieces of silver. And the Lord said to me, **"Throw it to the potter"**—the handsome price at which they valued me! So I took the **thirty pieces of silver** and **threw them to the potter** at the house of the Lord.

Matthew 26:14-15 Then one of the Twelve—the one called Judas Iscariot—went to the chief priests and asked, "What are you willing to give me if I deliver him over to you?" So they counted out for him **thirty pieces of silver**.

Matthew 27:3-10 When Judas, who had betrayed him, saw that Jesus was condemned, he was seized with remorse and returned the **thirty pieces of silver** to the chief priests and the elders. "I have sinned," he said, "for I have betrayed innocent blood."

"What is that to us?" they replied. "That's your responsibility."

So Judas threw the money into the temple and left. Then he went away and hanged himself. The chief priests picked up the coins and said, "It is against the law to put this into the treasury, since it is blood money." So **they decided to use the money to buy the potter's field** as a burial place for foreigners.

8. His death would be as a sacrificial lamb.
– Isaiah 53:5-8,10-11 (700 BC) fulfilled in John 1:29.

Isaiah 53:5-8 But he was **pierced for our transgressions**, he was crushed for our iniquities; the punishment that brought us peace was on him, and by his wounds we are healed. We all, like sheep, have gone astray, each of us has turned to our own way; and the **Lord has laid on him the iniquity of us all**. He was oppressed and afflicted, yet he did not open his mouth; he was led like a lamb to the slaughter, and as a sheep before its shearers is silent, so he did not open his mouth. By oppression and judgment he was taken away. Yet who of his generation protested? For he was cut off from the land of the living; **for the transgression of my people he was punished.**

John 1:29 The next day John saw Jesus coming toward him and said, "Look, the Lamb of God, who **takes away the sin of the world**!

9. Lots would be cast for his garment.
– Psalm 22:18 (1000 BC) fulfilled in John 19:23-24.

Psalm 22:18 They **divide my clothes among them and cast lots for my garment**.

John 19:23-24 When the soldiers crucified Jesus, they **took his clothes, dividing them** into four shares, one for each of them, with the undergarment remaining. This garment was seamless, woven in one piece from top to bottom. "Let's not tear it," they said to one another. **"Let's decide by lot who will get it."** This happened that the scripture might be fulfilled that said, "They divided my clothes among them and cast lots for my garment." So this is what the soldiers did.

10. **Death by crucifixion: hands and feet pierced.**
– Psalm 22:16 (1000 BC) fulfilled in Matthew 27:38.

Psalm 22:16 Dogs surround me, a pack of villains encircles me; they **pierce my hands and my feet**.

John 20:25 So the other disciples told him, "We have seen the Lord!" But he said to them, "Unless I see the **nail marks in his hands** and put my finger where the nails were, and put my hand into his side, I will not believe."

11. **The words spoken by those mocking him at his death.**
– Psalm 22:7,8 (1000 BC) fulfilled in Matthew 27:42-43.

Psalm 22:7,8 All who see me mock me; they hurl insults, shaking their heads. **"He trusts in the Lord," they say, "let the Lord rescue him. Let him deliver him, since he delights in him."**

Matthew 27:42-43 "He saved others," they said, "but he can't save himself! He's the king of Israel! Let him come down now from the cross, and we will believe in him. **He trusts in God. Let God rescue him now if he wants him**, for he said, 'I am the Son of God.'"

12. He would be buried in a rich man's tomb.
– Isaiah 53:9 (700 BC) fulfilled in Matthew 27:57-60.

Isaiah 53:9 He was **assigned a grave with the wicked, and with the rich in his death**, though he had done no violence, nor was any deceit in his mouth.

Matthew 27:57-60 As evening approached, there came **a rich man from Arimathea**, named Joseph, who had himself become a disciple of Jesus. Going to Pilate, he asked for Jesus' body, and Pilate ordered that it be given to him. Joseph **took the body, wrapped it in a clean linen cloth, and placed it in his own new tomb** that he had cut out of the rock.

13. He would return to life.
– Psalm 16:10 (1000 BC); Isaiah 53:10-11 (700 BC) fulfilled in Matthew 28:5-6.

Psalm 16:10 For You will **not abandon my soul to Sheol**; **Nor will You allow Your Holy One to undergo decay**.

Isaiah 53:10-11 Yet it was the Lord's will to crush him and cause him to suffer, and though the Lord **makes his life an offering for sin**, he will see his offspring and **prolong his days**, and the will of the Lord will prosper in his hand. **After he has suffered**, **he will see the light of life** and be satisfied; by his knowledge my righteous servant will justify many, and he will bear their iniquities.

Matthew 28:5-6 The angel said to the women, "Do not be afraid, for I know that you are looking for Jesus, who was crucified. He is not here; **he has risen**, just as he said. Come and see the place where he lay."

14. **He would be Light to the Gentiles.**
– Isaiah 42:1; Isaiah 49:6 (700 BC) fulfilled in Luke 2:29-32.

Isaiah 42:1 "Here is my servant, whom I uphold, my chosen one in whom I delight; I will put my Spirit on him, and he will bring justice **to the nations**."

Isaiah 49:6 he says: "It is too small a thing for you to be my servant to restore the tribes of Jacob   and bring back those of Israel I have kept. I will also make you a **light for the Gentiles**, that my salvation may reach to the ends of the earth."

Luke 2:29-32 "Sovereign Lord, as you have promised, you may now dismiss your servant in peace. For my eyes have seen your salvation, which you have prepared in the sight of **all nations**: **a light for revelation to the Gentiles**, and the glory of your people Israel."

15. **He would bring a new testament or covenant.**
– Jeremiah 31:31 (600 BC) fulfilled in Luke 22:20.

Jeremiah 31:31 "The days are coming," declares the Lord, "when I will **make a new covenant** with the people of Israel and with the people of Judah."

Luke 22:20 In the same way, after the supper he took the cup, saying, "This cup is the **new covenant in my blood**, which is poured out for you."

For more about the Christian community, see
www.sichurchofchrist.com

MAYBE YOU HAVE THOUGHT ABOUT BECOMING A CHRISTIAN

What Will You Do?

Suppose you saw a homeless man reach out his hand and raise a dead person to life and speak to a violent storm and command it to be calm, and you saw it happen.
What would you think?

You heard the same man teach people to love their enemies and to care for the poor. You saw him feed 5,000 hungry people starting with just five loaves and two fishes with 12 baskets of food left over after the meal. After that, you saw the man beaten and killed by his enemies, and then you saw him alive again a few days later.
What would you think?

His first followers said he is the creator of the universe, that his death was an act of divine love to take away the sins of all who come to him, and that he promised never-ending life to all who follow. The last time they saw him, he was taken up into the sky, and they reported that angels appeared who said he would return the same way he left.
What do you think? What will you do?
Contact collegemhc@gmail.com

23

The Way of the Cross
On Pain and Suffering

It is an honour to suffer because we know it is a small bit of what Christ suffered, and it is a way of sharing His suffering. Only Christianity provides this approach to suffering because only Jesus Christ suffered and died for humanity.

I was able to endure excruciating pain by **visualizing the suffering of Jesus on the cross** and realizing my suffering was much less than His suffering. My suffering was painful, and it was like His suffering in some way, yet my suffering was so much less than His suffering. Strange as it sounds, I welcomed the painful spasms as an opportunity to go to the cross and in a way to join the suffering of Christ. I did not try to make the spasms happen, but when they came, I could endure them as an honour to share even a small part of what His suffering must have been like.

Addiction can be overcome by accepting the suffering required to resist temptation as Jesus faced temptation in the desert. One can face death in the same way, looking to Him who suffered and died for us.

And he said to all, "If anyone would come after me, let him **deny himself and take up his cross daily** and follow me." - Luke 9:23

Then Pilate took Jesus and had him **flogged.** The soldiers twisted together a **crown of thorns and put it on his head.** They clothed him in a purple robe and went up to him again and again, saying, "Hail, king of the Jews!" And they **slapped him in the face.** - John 19:1-3

There they **nailed him** to the cross. - John 19:18

I am poured out like water, and **all my bones are out of joint. My heart has turned to wax;** it has melted within me. My **mouth is dried up** like a potsherd, and my **tongue sticks to the roof of my mouth;** you lay me in the **dust of death.** - Psalm 22:14-15

his appearance was **so disfigured beyond that of any human being** and **his form marred beyond human likeness** - Isaiah 52:14

But the LORD has caused the iniquity of us all to fall on Him. He was **oppressed and afflicted....**
- Isaiah 53:6-7

Going a little farther, he **fell with his face to the ground and prayed,** "My Father, if it is possible, may this cup be taken from me. Yet not as I will...." - Matthew 26:39

And in **His anguish,** He prayed more earnestly, and His **sweat became like drops of blood** falling to the ground.
- Luke 22:44

Because **he himself suffered** when he was tempted, he is able to help those who are being tempted. - Hebrews 2:18

I consider that **our present sufferings** are not worth comparing with the glory that will be revealed in us.
- Romans 8:28

that I may know Him and the power of His resurrection and **the fellowship of His sufferings,** being **conformed to His death;** in order that I may attain to the resurrection from the dead. - Philippians 3:10

Blessed be the God and Father of our Lord Jesus Christ, the Father of mercies and God of all comfort, who comforts us in all our affliction, so that we may be able to comfort those who are in **any affliction**, with the comfort with which we ourselves are comforted by God. For as **we share abundantly in Christ's sufferings**, so through Christ we share abundantly in comfort too. If we are afflicted, it is for your comfort and salvation; and if we are comforted, it is for your comfort, which you experience when you patiently endure the same sufferings that we suffer. Our hope for you is unshaken, for we know that as you share in our sufferings, you will also share in our comfort. - 2 Corinthians 1:3-7

always carrying about in the body the dying of Jesus, so that the life of Jesus also may be manifested in our body. For we who live are constantly being delivered over to death for Jesus' sake, so that the life of Jesus also may be manifested in our mortal flesh - 2 Corinthians 4:10-11

Consider it pure joy, my brothers and sisters, **whenever you face trials** of many kinds... - James 1:2

Blessed is the man who remains **steadfast under trial,** for when he has stood the test he will receive the crown of life, which God has promised to those who love him.
- James 1:12

For I am sure that neither death nor life, nor angels nor rulers, nor things present nor things to come, nor powers, nor height nor depth, nor anything else in all creation, will be able to separate us from the love of God in Christ Jesus our Lord. - Romans 8:39

And **after you have suffered a little while**, the God of all grace, who has called you to his eternal glory in Christ, will himself restore, confirm, strengthen, and establish you.
- 1 Peter 5:10

For we know that if the tent that is our earthly home is destroyed, we have a building from God, a house not made with hands, eternal in the heavens. For **in this tent we groan**, longing to put on our heavenly dwelling...
- 2 Corinthians 5:1-2

Now **I rejoice in what I am suffering** for you, and I fill up in my flesh what is still lacking in regard to Christ's afflictions, for the sake of his body, which is the church.
- Colossians 1:24

Not only that, but **we rejoice in our sufferings**, knowing that **suffering** produces endurance, and endurance produces character, and character produces hope...
- Romans 5:3-4

Love

The kind of love in the following passages is undeserved or unconditional favour. This is the love God had for the world in giving Jesus to be a sacrifice for sin. This love prefers to die rather than to kill because it is sacrificial in imitation of the love of Jesus in taking on the sins of the world in his suffering and death. It is the love we must have for everyone, and it is the foundation of healthy relationships with self and others. Protecting the innocent against the unjust assailant, and if all nonviolent means fail, may require the death of the follower of Jesus who died for his enemies.

Matthew 5:44, 46 – **love your enemies**....there is no value in loving those who love you.

Matthew 19:19; 22:39 – **love your neighbor** as yourself.

Luke 6:27-32 – love, bless, do good, pray **for enemies**.

John 3:16 - For **God so loved** the world that he gave his one and only Son, that whoever believes in him shall not perish but have eternal life.

John 13:34 – love one another.

John 14:23 - Jesus replied, "**Anyone who loves me will obey** my teaching. My Father will love them, and **we will come to them and make our home with them."**

John 15:12, 17 – **love one another.**

John 15:13 – greater love has no man than to **lay down his life** for his friend.

Romans 5:5 - hope does not put us to shame, because **God's love has been poured out into our hearts** through the Holy Spirit.

Romans 5:8 - **God demonstrates His own love toward us,** in that while we were yet sinners, Christ died for us.

Romans 12:9 - **let love be genuine.**

Romans 13:8 – **owe no one anything but to love.**

Romans 13:10 - **love does no wrong** to a neighbor; therefore love is the fulfilling of the law.

1 Corinthians 13:4-7 – **love is patient and kind**, is not irritable or resentful... bears all things, endures all things.

1 Corinthians 16:14 – let **all things be done in love**.

Galatians 5:13 – **by love serve** one another.

Galatians 5:22 – love is **fruit of the Spirit**.

Ephesians 4:2 – **bearing with one another in love**.

Ephesians 5:2 – **Live a life of love just as Christ loved us** and gave himself for us as a sweet-smelling offering and sacrifice to God.

Colossians 3:12-14 - Therefore, as God's chosen people, holy and dearly loved, clothe yourselves with **compassion, kindness, humility, gentleness and patience**. Bear with each other and **forgive one another** if any of you has a grievance against someone. Forgive as the Lord forgave you. And **over all these virtues put on love**, which binds them all together in perfect unity.

1 Thessalonians 3:12 - **May the Lord make your love increase** and overflow for each other and **for everyone else**, just as ours does for you.

1 Peter 2:17 – **love the brotherhood**.

1 John 2:15 – **love not** things in the world.

1 John 3:16,17 – **love is to give** to the needs of others and to lay down one's life.

1 John 4:9-11 – By this the **love of God** was manifested in us, that God has sent His only begotten Son into the world so that we might live through Him. In **this is love**, not that we loved God, but that **He loved us and sent His Son** to be the sacrifice for our sins. Beloved, if God so loved us, **we also ought to love one another**.

The Love of God: A Meditation
The Heart and Message of the Cross

And so we know and rely on the love God has for us. God is love.
Whoever lives in love lives in God, and God in them. – 1 John 4:16

Christians possess the most powerful weapon against terrorism and violence. That weapon is love! Yet we do not know how to use this love. We use love by dying for our enemies just as our Leader died for us when we were his enemies when he could have destroyed us.

And he called unto him the multitude with his disciples, and said unto them, If any man would come after me, let him **deny himself, and take up his cross,** and follow me. - Mark 8:24

God's love has been poured out into our hearts through the Holy Spirit, who has been given to us.
- Romans 5:5

But **God demonstrates his own love for us** in this: While **we were still sinners, Christ died** for us.
- Romans 5:8

Therefore, since we have now been justified by His blood, how much more shall we be saved from wrath through Him! - Romans 5:9

For if, **while we were God's enemies,** we were **reconciled to him through the death of his Son,** how much more, having been reconciled, shall we be saved through his life! - Romans 5:10

The Heart of the Cross

When judged, we may tend to judge in return. How can we transform our judgment and condemnation of others into caring and compassion for them? What does the cross teach us?

At the heart of our faith is the cross, and at **the heart of the cross is the love of God** who suffered for our offenses. The cross teaches us to love and care for those who offend us. This kind of love is so against our emotional and cultural custom that sometimes we can't see it. We can't grasp it. The next time you are offended, remember these words:

John 3:16 For **God so loved the world** that he gave his one and only Son...

Romans 5:5 And hope does not put us to shame, because **God's love has been poured out into our hearts** through the Holy Spirit, who has been given to us.

Romans 5:8-10 But **God demonstrates his own love for us** in this: While we were still sinners, Christ died for us. Since we have now been justified by his blood, how much more shall we be saved from God's wrath through him! For if, while we were God's enemies, we were reconciled to him through the death of his Son

2 Thessalonians 3:5 Now may the **Lord direct your hearts into the love of God** and into the patience of Christ.

Ephesians 5:1-2 Follow God's example, therefore, **as dearly loved children and walk in the way of love, just as Christ**

loved us and gave himself up for us as a fragrant offering and sacrifice to God.

1 John 3:16 This is **how we know what love is: Jesus Christ laid down his life for us**. And we ought to lay down our lives for our brothers and sisters.

1 John 4:10 **This is love: not that we loved God, but that he loved us and sent his Son as an atoning sacrifice for our sins.**

1 John 4:19-21 **We love because he first loved us**.... Anyone who loves God must also love their brother and sister.

The prophet Isaiah (chapter 53) said of Christ, "By oppression and judgment he was taken away." Yet when Jesus was suffering mockery and condemnation on the cross, he said, "Father forgive them....." And Peter observed of Christ that "When they hurled their insults at him, **he did not retaliate; when he suffered, he made no threats.**"

2 Corinthians 13:11 Finally, brothers and sisters, rejoice! Strive for full restoration, encourage one another, be of one mind, live in peace. And **the God of love and peace** will be with you.

Nonviolence in Early Christian Thought

prepared by Daniel Keeran, MSW, Victoria, Canada
collegemhc@gmail.com

If nonviolence is the teaching of Jesus in the New Testanment, we would expect to find it in the earliest writings of Christians after the apostles and prophets of the Lord. What do we find?

First Century

Love your enemies – Luke 6:27-28 do good to those who hate you, bless those who curse you, pray for those who mistreat you.

But I tell you, do not resist an evil person. – Matthew 5:38-39 If anyone slaps you on the right cheek, turn to them the other cheek also.

Stephen stoned – Acts 7:54-60 when stoned to death, Stephen says "forgive them".

Christians dragged to prison and death - Acts 8:1-3, Acts 22:3-5, Acts 26:9-11, Galatians 1:13

James killed – Acts 12:1-3 was killed with the sword.

Paul threatened and arrested – Acts 28:19 had no charge to bring against those who conspired to kill him.

Christians treated violently – Romans 12:17- 21 overcome evil with good.

Christian slaves beaten for doing what is right – 1 Peter 2:18-25 suffer patiently as Christ did.

Do not fear suffering violent attack – 1 Peter 3:14-15, Rev.2:10 be faithful unto death.

Christians facing opposition were called to **have their own blood shed** – Heb.12:3-4.

Do not war as the world does but use your spiritual weapons – 2 Cor. 10:3-6, Eph.6:12-18.

The death of Jesus for His enemies (when He could have destroyed them) defines a new kind of love. – "This is love: not that we loved God, but that he loved us and sent his Son as an atoning sacrifice for our sins." – 1 John 4:10

Second to Fourth Century

Ignatius of Antioch (80-140 AD) in *Epistle to the Ephesians*: "And let us imitate the Lord, who, when He was reviled, reviled not again ; when He was crucified, He answered not; when He suffered, He threatened not ; but prayed for His enemies, Father, forgive them; they know not what they do. **If any one, the more he is injured, displays the more patience, blessed is he.**"

Justin Martyr (110-165 AD) in *Dialogue with Trypho*: "...we who were filled with war, and mutual slaughter, and every wickedness, have each through the whole earth **changed our warlike weapons**,— our swords into ploughshares, and our spears into implements of tillage, —and we cultivate piety, righteousness, philanthropy, faith, and hope..."

Irenaeus (120-202 AD) in *Against Heresies*: "But if the law of liberty, that is, the word of God, preached by the apostles (who went forth from Jerusalem) throughout all the earth, caused such **a change in the state of things**, that these [nations] **did form the swords and war-lances into ploughshares, and changed them into pruning-hooks for reaping the grain, [that is], into instruments used for peaceful purposes**, and that **they are now unaccustomed to fighting**, but when smitten, offer also the other cheek…"

Emperor Marcus Aurelius (121-180 AD) in Justin Martyr (100-165 AD), *First Apology*, *Ante-Nicene Fathers*: "The Emperor Caesar Marcus Aurelius, to the People of Rome, and to the sacred Senate… I was surrounded by the enemy; and the enemy being at hand… there was close on us a mass of a mixed multitude of 977,000 men, which indeed we saw… Having then examined my own position, and my host, with respect to… the enemy, I quickly betook myself to prayer to the gods of my country. But being disregarded by them, **I summoned those who among us go by the name of Christians**. And having made inquiry, I discovered a great number and vast host of them, and raged against them, which was by no means becoming; for afterwards I learned their power. Wherefore **they began the battle, not by preparing weapons, nor arms, nor bugles; for such preparation is hateful to them, on account of the God they bear about in their conscience.**" (Note: While the authenticity of the letter is disputed, scholars accept that even if it is a forgery, it was written in the latter part of the second century and therefore reflects the values and beliefs of Christians at that time.)

Athenagoras (about 170 AD) in *A Plea for the Christians*: "…for we have learned, not only not to return blow for blow, **nor to go to law with those who plunder and rob us**, but to those who smite us on one side of the face to offer the other side also, and to those who take away our coat to give likewise our cloak."

Clement of Alexandria (150-215 AD) in *Paedogogus*: "**In peace, not in war, we are trained**."

Clement of Alexandria in *Protrepticus*: "If you enroll as one of God's people, heaven is your country and God your lawgiver. And **what are His laws**? You shall not kill, You shall love your neighbor as yourself. **To him that strikes you on the one cheek, turn to him the other also**."

Tertullian (145-220 AD) in *On Idolatry*: "But **how will a Christian man war, nay, how will he serve even in peace, without a sword**, which the Lord has taken away? For albeit soldiers had come unto John, and had received the formula of their rule; albeit, likewise, a centurion had believed; still **the Lord afterward, in disarming Peter, unbelted every soldier**."

Hippolytus (170-235 AD) in *Apostolic Tradition*: "**Persons who possess authority to kill, or soldiers, should not kill at all, even when it is commanded of them**. Everyone who receives a distinctive leading position, or a magisterial power, and does not clothe himself in the weaponlessness of which is becoming to the Gospel, should be separated from the flock."

Hippolytus in *Canons*: "**No Christian should go and become a soldier** unless a commander who has a sword compels him; let him not draw any guilt of blood shed upon himself."

Origen (185-254 AD) in *Against Celsus*: "To those who inquire of us from where we come, or who is our founder, we reply that we have come agreeably to the counsels of Jesus. We have cut down our hostile, insolent, and wearisome swords into plowshares. We have converted into pruning hooks the spears that were formerly used in war. For we **no longer take up sword** against nation, nor do we learn war any more. That is because we have **become children of peace for the sake of Jesus, who is our leader**."

"**We do not indeed fight under him, although he require it**; but we fight on his behalf, forming a special army -- an army of piety -- by offering our prayers to God."

Arnobius (died 326 AD) in *Against the Heathen*: "A numerous band of men as we are, we have learned from his teaching and his laws that evil should not be repaid with evil. Rather, it is better to suffer wrong than to inflict it. We would **rather shed our own blood than stain our hands and our conscience with that of another**."

Lactantius (220-330 AD, tutor for the emperor Constantine's children) in *The Divine Institutes*:

"For how can a man be just who injures, who hates, who despoils, **who puts to death**? And **they who strive to be serviceable to their country** do all these things..."

"For when God forbids us to kill, He not only prohibits us from open violence, which is not even allowed by the public laws, but He warns us against the commission of those things which are esteemed lawful among men. Thus it will be **neither lawful for a just man to engage in warfare, since his warfare is justice itself**, nor to accuse any one of a capital charge, because it makes no difference whether you put a man to death by word, or rather by the sword, since it is the act of putting to death itself which is prohibited. Therefore, with regard to this precept of God, there ought to be no exception at all; but that it is always unlawful to put to death a man, whom God willed to be a sacred animal."

Martin of Tours (316-397 AD) in *The Paedagogus* - "I am a soldier of Christ. **To fight is not permissible for me.**"

Change in the 4th Century

Lactantius (see above) in *On the Death of the Persecutors*: "Constantine was **directed in a dream to cause the heavenly sign to be delineated on the shields of his soldiers**, and so to proceed to battle."

Eusebius (260-339 AD) in *The Life of the Blessed Emperor Constantine*: "Then, in his sleep, the Christ of God appeared to him with the same sign which he had seen in the heavens and commanded him to make a likeness of that sign which he had seen in the heavens and to use it as a safeguard **in all engagements with his enemies.**"

Ambrose (340-397 AD, teacher of Augustine) in *Duties of Ministers*: "For the **fortitude which in war defends the fatherland from barbarians** or defends the weak at home, or companions from thieves is full of justice."

Augustine (354-430 AD) in *Epistle 189, To Boniface, A Soldier*: "Do not think that no one can please God who is a soldier in military arms. Holy David was among these, to whom the Lord gave such great witness [see 1 Kings 14.7, where God says David, "followed me with all his heart, doing only what was right in my eyes:] and many just men of that time among them. Among these was Cornelius [Acts 10] to whom the angel was sent.... Among these were those   who came to

John for baptism.... **Surely he did not forbid them to serve in arms**, to whom he ordered to be content with their pay.
....Some therefore fight for you by praying against   invisible enemies; you work for them **by fighting against visible barbarians**.... So think first of this, **when you arm yourself for battle**, that even your bodily strength is a gift of God...."

Related

http://www.amazon.com/Concordance-Testament-Christian-Pacifism-Nonviolence/dp/1499186436

http://www.amazon.com/Radical-Christianity-Peace-Justice-Testament/dp/0973454652

Decisions for the Poor

In recent decades, a number of benevolent organizations and non-religious efforts, have made extensive appeals for contributions from the public. Undoubtedly, we will see more presentations of this kind as world population increases and as the gap widens between rich and poor nations. Every Christian must now ask this question, "What does God expect of *me* in view of the millions who are starving right now?"

Good News for the Poor

To answer this question, we will begin with a Messianic passage found in Isaiah 11, verse 4: "With righteousness he will judge the needy, with justice he will give decisions for the poor of the earth." One of the primary ministries of the Messiah was to bless the poor. The place of rich and poor in relation to the Messianic kingdom is introduced by Mary's magnification of God and by the first preaching of John the Baptist and of the Christ himself.

Mary affirms that God has "scattered those who are proud in their inmost thoughts" and that he has brought down the powerful and "sent the rich away empty." Moreover, she declares, God has "lifted up the humble" and has "filled the hungry with good things" (Luke 1:51-54).

When John the Baptist appears, he refers to Isaiah 40:3-5 as his program of ministry. John understands that his purpose is to prepare the way of the Lord by a type of landscaping that brings down mountains and hills while the valleys are exalted or filled in. This is reminiscent of Mary's statement, for when the multitude inquire about the proper fruit of repentance, mountains and hills are lowered and valleys are exalted as John instructs the people to distribute their abundance to the poor. Even specific groups among the crowd are divested of their lucrative incomes as John exhorts soldiers and tax collectors to cease extortion, to collect only the tax due, and to be content with meager wages (Luke 3:4-14). The powerful and rich are brought down and sent empty away while the poor and humble are filled with good things and lifted up, even as Mary had declared concerning the justice of God.

When Jesus appears, he refers to Isaiah 61:1,2 as his program of ministry. Jesus understands that he is "anointed to bring good news to the poor" (Luke 4:18ff). Since the term "Messiah" actually means "anointed one," Jesus is announcing that good news for the poor is at the very heart of his teaching and preaching ministry. Jesus corroborates the statement of Isaiah 11:4 that he will make "decisions for the poor of the earth." In fact, the proof for the imprisoned John that Jesus was indeed the expected Messiah was that Jesus was fulfilling the prophecy of Isaiah 61: 1,2, for he was blessing the afflicted and preaching the Gospel to the poor (Luke 7:21, 22).

The Gospel message of Jesus to the poor themselves is this: "Blessed are you who are poor, for yours is the kingdom of God" (Luke 6:20). These are not the spiritually poor but the literally poor, for in the same address Jesus pronounces a woe upon the literally rich (v. 24). That the poor filled the kingdom is verified by James 2:5: "Listen, my dear brothers: has not God chosen those who are poor in the eyes to world to be rich in faith and to inherit the kingdom he promised to those who love him?" It is not surprising that James again echoes Jesus in pronouncing the strongest condemnation on the rich: "Come now, you rich, weep and wail because of the misery that is coming upon you" (James 5:1).

A Costly Response Demanded

The message of the New Testament to the rich demands a costly response, for the rich enter the kingdom and benefit from the Gospel only as servants of the poor. This is clear from the very beginning of the preaching of the Gospel of the kingdom, for those who have must distribute to those who have not, in order to receive John's baptism (Luke 3:10-11).

To all his disciples Jesus says, "Lay not up treasure on earth...but lay up for yourselves treasure in heaven" (Matt. 6:19f). To the little flock Jesus explains how treasure is laid up in heaven: "Sell what you have and give to the poor" (Luke 12:33). The rich young ruler was given the same instruction: "Sell your possessions and give to the poor, and you will have treasure in heaven" (Matt. 19:21). To the Pharisees, Jesus declared, "Give what you have to the poor, and all will be clean for you" (Luke 11:41). The mandate of Jesus' earthly ministry is clear: in order to be assured of eternal life, heavenly treasure, spiritual cleanness, the rich must distribute their abundance to the poor.

Zaccheus, the rich tax collector, received salvation - treasure in heaven - by responding to this new ethic of the Messianic kingdom. He made a commitment to distribute his wealth to the poor and to those whom he had oppressed. Surely, by the time he had kept his promise to restore four-fold to those he had wronged, Zaccheus would find himself among those to whom the kingdom belongs (Luke 19:8,9). Because of the radical response of Zaccheus, we can infer that he had heard Jesus preaching a radical commitment in terms of distributing one's wealth to the poor.

Indeed, those who store up treasure for themselves on earth rather than distributing to the poor are like the rich fool of whom Jesus speaks. To sacrifice one's affluence for the poor is to be "rich toward God" (Luke 12:21; Matt. 25:40). The rich do not give abundantly and acceptably until they give as the widow who gave all she had (Mark 12:41f). This teaching from the account of the widow's mite should be regarded as providing the definition of liberality and "sowing abundantly," as Paul later enjoins (II Cor.9:6). The widow, however, was not resigned to death by starvation, for her support came from the temple treasury, but her degree of giving reinforces what Jesus has said about the obligation of the rich to give out of their need level, which means all of their abundance and then some.

In the parable of the unjust steward Jesus teaches powerfully that to withhold God's trust of worldly wealth from those in need is embezzlement, and the consequence is to be denied true riches. "I tell you," he said, "use worldly wealth to gain friends for yourselves, so that when it is gone, you will be welcomed into eternal dwellings" (Luke 16:8-12).

Jesus then immediately gives warning to the wise in the illustration of the rich man and Lazarus. The fate of the rich man who failed to come to terms with worldly wealth illustrated Jesus' pronouncement of woe upon the rich, for they have already received their comfort in this life (Luke 16:19-25; 6:24). The rich man died and was refused entrance into eternal dwellings. His worldly wealth was gone, and he had not been trustworthy.

It is in the context of what is said in the parable of the unjust steward, illustrated again by the rich man and Lazarus, that we must understand Jesus' teaching about serving two masters. Serving God is using "worldly wealth to gain friends," thus being "trustworthy with someone else's [God's] property"(Luke 16:9,12). Serving mammon or wealth is withholding God's trust from the poor, preferring rather to live in luxury and comfort in a world of suffering and want (Luke 16: 19-25).

The injunction to distribute one's abundance makes it impossible to keep God's property for self and maintain trust in God. This is the meaning of Jesus' statement that "you cannot serve God and wealth" (Luke 16:13). He who chooses to keep God's possessions, has despised God and his will for the affluent: "What is highly valued among men is detestable in God's sight" (Luke 16:15). Giving, not out of one's wealth, but out of one's need, is the teaching of the Kingdom from the words of John the Baptist to the widow who gave a fraction of a penny.

A universal principle of discipleship is stated in Luke 14:33: "Any of you who does not give up everything he has cannot be my disciple." Jesus is calling upon prospective followers to forsake, relinquish, or renounce the possession of earthly goods.

46

He is not here speaking of family relationships as in verse 26, because the Greek phrase for "everything he has" refers to literal material possessions or earthly goods. "The expression always (fourteen times) denotes earthly goods in the New Testament" (G. Kittel, ed., *Theological Dictionary of the New Testament*, Vol. 8, p. 33). The same principle is stated in other words when Jesus commends laying up heavenly treasure instead of, not in addition to, earthly treasure (Matt. 6:19).

Generosity of Early Christians

Not only does this emphasis pervade the Gospel accounts, but it is also found throughout the New Testament. The immediate response of the first Christians was to determine that all things would be held as common property. This meant that they sold their possessions and gave to the poor. The result was that no one among them was in need (Acts 2:44, 45; 4:32, 34, 35). Ananias and Sapphira felt compelled to do what was being done by others: selling and giving. Laying the money at the apostles' feet was not compulsory, but was simply one method of distribution. Yet there was perhaps a degree of status attached to the act, at least in the minds of this couple, who were prompted to go so far as to lie about having given all (Acts 4:32- 5:11).

Eventually during a long famine, the saints in Jerusalem had spent their resources. Paul then tried to encourage the same kind of giving from the Corinthians as had occurred earlier in Jerusalem, suggesting that the sincerity of one's love in giving is to be measured or defined by the example of the Macedonians, who gave out of "their extreme poverty" (II Cor. 8:2), and by the example of Christ himself, who "though he was rich, yet for your sakes he became poor..." (v.9).

Paul does not want to command or compel the Corinthians to give in this way, because he wants them to be willing and cheerful in their giving (II Cor. 8:12; 9:7). Yet the expectation is clear in terms of the degree of giving Paul wants from them, for he continues by urging, "At the present time your plenty will supply what they need... as it is written, he that gathered much did not have too much, and he that gathered little did not have too little" (II Cor. 8:14,15). Further, Paul emphasizes the importance of sowing generously, defined by the preceding examples of Macedonia and of Christ, which reflect Jesus' definition of abundant giving in the example of the poor widow who gave more than the rich because she gave what she needed to live on.

The Source and Purpose of Wealth

Paul identifies God as the source of one's abundance, and the purpose of God's gift is two-fold: (1) to provide for the needs of the one who receives from God, and (2) to allow the one who receives to provide for the needs of others (Acts 20:34-35; Eph. 4:28). The rich have received from God, not to increase their enjoyment of luxury and comfort, but to increase their distribution unto "every good work" and so they "can be generous on every occasion." It is through the generosity of the rich that God "has scattered abroad his gifts to the poor" (II Cor. 9:8-11). When the rich neglect to do this, they have embezzled God's gifts and fail in their servant role.

In his first letter to Timothy, Paul suggests that generosity and good deeds enable one to lay up treasure in heaven – reminiscent of Jesus' instruction to the little flock, the rich young ruler, and all disciples (Matt. 6:19ff). Notice that rather than being rich in the possession of wealth, the affluent are to be rich in the giving of those possessions (1 Tim. 6:17-19). Certainly, Paul could not have meant less than Jesus meant in his definition of generosity.

John makes a similar point. Those who live in luxury and abundance in spite of the suffering of the poor do not have God's love within them (I John 3:16,17). While John emphasizes this responsibility to the poor brother, the New Testament extends the demonstration of love to all men (Gal. 6:10; II Cor. 9:13; I Thess. 3:12). The love and grace of Christ find reality in the believer's life in sacrificing possessions as Christ did (I John 3:16; II Cor. 8:9).

Giving as the Macedonians, Christ, and the poor widow gave, will reduce us to a simple life style, with basic necessities and minimal possessions (I Tim. 6:8). Luxury and self-indulgence are among the sins of the rich (James 5:5). Christians are specifically forbidden to wear expensive clothes and jewelry (I Pet. 3:3; I Tim. 2:9-10). According to Jesus, those who have already received their comfort in this life will find no comfort in the next life (Luke 6:24; 16:19-25). But those who are caring and generous can know the blessedness of giving (Acts 20:35) and the assurance of the Lord's promise never to abandon us (Heb. 13:5).

In the book of Revelation, the church of Laodicea claims to be rich and in need of nothing because of her accumulated wealth. But Jesus assesses her situation differently: "You do not realize that you are wretched, pitiful, poor, blind and naked. I counsel you to buy from me gold refined in the fire, so you can become rich" (Rev. 3:17-18). One can convert earthly riches into "gold refined in the fire" by distributing one's wealth to the poor.

The Abominations of Babylon

The abominations of Babylon the Great are a final reminder of the thesis of this study. The rich and powerful are intimately associated with the sinful city. "The kings of the earth committed adultery with her, and the merchants of the earth grew rich from her excessive luxuries" (Rev. 18:3). God's people must not share in her sins (v. 4). She will receive "as much torture and grief as the glory and luxury she gave herself" (v. 7). In her day of judgment, Babylon the Great will mourn with all those who became rich through her wealth (v. 7,9,19). Here we see fulfilled the truth of Jesus' words: "Woe to you who are rich, for you have already received your comfort" (Luke 6:24).

Moreover, Mary's words at the beginning of the New Testament are strangely fulfilled in this closing vision of Babylon, for the rich and powerful are brought down and sent empty away. In Babylon is seen the fate of all who live in luxury at the expense or neglect of the world's poor. On the other hand, God's faithful poor and those who distribute their wealth according to God's purpose can look forward to the comfort and luxury of the New Jerusalem, the heavenly treasure for those who have invested wisely.

Attitudes of the Early Church

Isaiah promised Messianic decisions for the poor, and we have seen their fulfillment in the words of Mary, John the Baptist, the Messiah himself, Paul, James, the apostle John, and in the deeds of the Jerusalem and Macedonian churches.

The early church writers from the close of the New Testament through the time of Constantine soundly support the biblical teaching concerning the place of rich and poor in the kingdom of God. Clement of Rome (96 A.D.) observed that many Christians had sold themselves into slavery in order to buy food for others. Aristides (120 A.D.) pointed out that early Christians fasted in order to send their food to the poor (see *Apology* 15). The Shepherd of Hermas (136 A.D.) affirmed that God gave abundance to the rich so that they could spend their wealth and "all their possessions" to relieve others (see *Similitudes,* I:8f). In the *Epistle to Diognetus,* 10:4,5 (140 A.D.) the affluent are instructed to distribute the things received from God, to help those in need. In the *Preaching of Peter* (180 A.D.) it is said that the abundance of the rich belongs to the poor. Clement of Alexandria (190 A.D.) said it is not right for one to live in luxury while others are in want (see *Instructor* II.xiii.20:6).

In *Against Heresies*, IV.xiv.3, Irenaeus (180 A.D.) expressed the following: "And instead of the tithes which the Law commanded, the Lord said to divide everything we have with the poor." (See the chapter entitled, "Early Christian Acts of Mercy," in Everett Ferguson's *Early Christians Speak*, Austin: Sweet, 1971).

Conclusion

The values of the kingdom with regard to wealth have remained obscure amid the "pursuit of happiness." Perhaps this is partly because those whose salaries are paid by the wealthy, have sought to please and accommodate the rich. If so, the advice given to the church of Laodicea is appropriate for us. We must obtain gold from our Lord that we may become truly rich. We must flee from the destruction of Babylon and partake in her sins no longer. May God help us as we seek always to have less of this world that we may possess more of the kingdom of God. We will realize more of his Kingdom when we have lived by his "decisions for the poor of the earth."

Jesus and the Early Church on Wealth:
The Most Avoided Teaching

HOW TO BECOME A CHRISTIAN
WWW.BOX.COM/LOVEGOD

Mark 12:43-44 Calling his disciples to him, Jesus said, I tell you the truth, **this poor widow has put more into the treasury than all the others**. They all gave out of their wealth; but she, out of her poverty, put in everything--all she had to live on.

Luke 1:53 He has **filled the hungry** with good things but has sent the rich away empty.

Luke 3:11 John answered, Anyone who has **two shirts should share** with the one who has none, and anyone who has food should do the same.

Luke 4:18-19 The Spirit of the Lord is on me, because he has anointed me to proclaim **good news to the poor**. He has sent me to proclaim freedom for the prisoners and recovery of sight for the blind, to set the oppressed free, to proclaim the year of the Lord's favour. Then he rolled up the scroll, gave it back to the attendant and sat down. The eyes of everyone in the synagogue were fastened on him. He began by saying to them, Today this scripture is fulfilled in your hearing.

Luke 6:20 Looking at his disciples, he said, Blessed are you who are **poor, for yours is the kingdom** of God.

Luke 6:24 But **woe to you who are rich**, for you have already received your comfort.

Luke 6:38 Give, and it will be given to you. A good measure, pressed down, shaken together and running over, will be poured into your lap. For **with the measure you use, it will be measured to you**.

Luke 7:22 So he replied to the messengers, "Go back and report to John what you have seen and heard: The blind receive sight, the lame walk, those who have leprosy are cleansed, the deaf hear, the dead are raised, and the **good news is proclaimed to the poor**."

Matt. 6:19 Lay not up treasure on earth...but lay up for yourselves treasure in heaven.

Matt. 19:21 Sell your possessions and give to the poor, and you will have treasure in heaven.

Matt. 19:24 Again I tell you, it is **easier for a camel** to go through the eye of a needle than for a rich man to enter the kingdom of God.

Luke 18:22 You still lack one thing. **Sell everything you have and give to the poor**, and you will have treasure in heaven. Then come, follow me.

Luke 11:41 Give what you have to the poor, and all will be clean for you.

Luke 12:19-21 And I'll say to myself: 'Take life easy; eat, drink and be merry.' But God said to him, 'You fool! This very night your life will be demanded from you. Then who will get what you have prepared for yourself?' This is how it will be with whoever stores up things for themselves but is not rich toward God."

Luke 14:12-14 When you give a luncheon or dinner, do not invite your friends, your brothers or relatives, or your rich neighbours; if you do, they may invite you back and so you will be repaid. But when you give a banquet, **invite the poor**, the crippled, the lame, the blind, and you will be blessed. Although they cannot repay you, you will be repaid at the resurrection of the righteous.

Luke 14:33 Any of you who does not **give up everything he has** cannot be my disciple.

Luke 16:8-12 I tell you, he said, **use worldly wealth to gain friends** for yourselves, so that when it is gone, you will be welcomed into eternal dwellings.

Luke 16:19,25 There was a certain rich man, who was clothed in purple and fine linen, and fared sumptuously every day....But Abraham replied, Son, remember that in your lifetime you received your good things, while Lazarus (the beggar) received bad things, but now **he is comforted here and you are in agony**.

Acts 2:44-45 All the believers were together and had everything in common. They sold property and possessions to **give to anyone who had need**.

2 Cor. 8:9 For you know the grace of our Lord Jesus Christ, that though he was rich, yet for your sakes **he became poor**, so that you through his poverty might become rich.

2 Cor. 9:8-9 And God is able to bless you abundantly, so that in all things at all times, having all that you need, you will **abound in every good work**. As it is written: "They have freely scattered their **gifts to the poor**; their righteousness endures forever."

1 Timothy 6:8 But if we have **food and clothing**, we will be content with that.

1 Timothy 6:17-19 Command those who are rich in this present world not to be arrogant nor to put their hope in wealth, which is so uncertain, but to put their hope in God, who richly provides us with everything for our enjoyment. Command them to do good, to be **rich in good deeds, and to be generous and willing to share**. In this way they will lay up treasure for themselves as a firm foundation for the coming age, so that they may take hold of the life that is truly life.

Hebrews 13:5 Keep your lives free from the love of money and **be content with what you have**, because God has said, "Never will I leave you; never will I forsake you."

James 1:9,10 The brother in humble circumstances ought to take pride in his high position. But the one who is **rich should take pride in his low position**, because he will pass away like a wild flower.

James 2:5 "Listen, my dear brothers: has not **God chosen those who are poor** in the eyes of the world to be rich in faith and to inherit the kingdom he promised to those who love him?"

James 5:1 Now listen, **you rich people**, weep and wail because of the misery that is coming upon you.

Early Church Sources

Clement of Rome (96 A.D.) said he knew of many who had sold themselves into slavery in order to use the money to feed the hungry, and some had **sold themselves into bondage** to purchase freedom for others (Clement, Epistle to the Corinthians, 55:2).

Shepherd of Hermas (135 A.D.) "Therefore instead of fields, purchase afflicted souls, as each is able. And visit widows and orphans and do not neglect them. Spend your wealth and all your possessions on such 'fields and houses' which you receive from God. For **the master made you rich for this purpose** that you might perform these ministries for him" (Similitudes, I:8f).

Preaching of Peter (140 A.D.) "Understand then you rich, that you are in **duty bound to do service**, having received more than you yourselves need. Learn that to others is lacking that wherein you superabound. Be ashamed of holding fast what belongs to others. Imitate God's equity and none shall be poor."

Against Heresies, IV.xiv.3, Irenaeus (180 A.D.) "And instead of the tithes which the Law commanded, the

Lord said to divide everything we have with the poor."

Clement of Alexandria (190 A.D.) "And it is **not right for one to live in luxury while others live in want**. How much more glorious is it to do good to many than to live sumptuously! How much wiser to spend money on human beings than on jewels and gold!" (Instructor II, xiii, 20.3 and 6).

HOW TO BECOME A CHRISTIAN
WWW.BOX.COM/LOVEGOD

Are the Teachings of Jesus Relevant Today?

The following is material presented by the author at a meeting of the Humanist Association in Victoria, British Columbia, Canada, November 6, 2011.

(Scripture quotes are from the New International Version)

Introduction: A young man in prison said he was an atheist when sentenced; he saw that people who lived by Jesus' teaching were stable and happy; he now thinks there may be a superior intelligence who gave the teaching.

Jesus did not come to bring an economic or political system but to transform the individual. He said: "My kingdom is not of this world," and "The kingdom of God is within you."

The teachings of Jesus provide the fundamental principles for the well-being of individuals and communities. Setting a high bar of behavioural expectation, these teachings are at the moral and social foundation of Western civilization. Beside the word **Relevance,** the applications of Jesus' teaching is given below the scripture passages organized in categories of social teachings, peace and nonviolence, and psychological well-being.

LUKE 6:20-42 (Sermon on the Plain)

Social Teachings
20,24,25 **Blessed are you who are poor**, for yours is the kingdom of God....But **woe to you who are rich**, for

you have already received your comfort. Woe to you who are well fed now, for you will go hungry.

Relevance: See the entire book of Luke for social teaching and care for the poor. Citizens of the kingdom must provide for those who cannot otherwise benefit from opportunities to sustain life.

37-38 "**Do not judge, and you will not be judged. Do not condemn, and you will not be condemned. Forgive, and you will be forgiven. Give, and it will be given to you.**

Relevance: Jesus provides principles to reduce conflict and live in harmony with others.

Peace and Nonviolence
27-29,35-36 "**Love your enemies, do good to those who hate you, bless those who curse you, pray for those who mistreat you**. If someone slaps you on one cheek, turn to them the other also.... But love your enemies, do good to them, and lend to them without expecting to get anything back. Then your reward will be great, and you will be children of the Most High, because he is kind to the ungrateful and wicked. Be merciful, just as your Father is merciful.

Relevance: This teaching was the core of the civil rights movement begun by Martin Luther King. Mahatma Gandhi, drawing the idea of nonviolent resistance from this teaching, said: "If Christians would really live according to the teachings of Christ, as found in the Bible, all of India would be Christian today."

MATTHEW: chapters 5-7 (Sermon on the Mount)

ch5- Psychological Well-Being

3-12 Blessed are the **poor in spirit**, for theirs is the kingdom of heaven. Blessed are **those who mourn**, for they will be comforted. Blessed are the meek, for they will inherit the earth. Blessed are those who hunger and thirst for **righteousness**, for they will be filled. Blessed are **the merciful**, for they will be shown mercy. Blessed are the **pure in heart**, for they will see God. Blessed are the **peacemakers**, for they will be called children of God. Blessed are those who are persecuted because of righteousness, for theirs is the kingdom of heaven. Blessed are you **when people insult you, persecute you and falsely say** all kinds of evil against you because of me.

Relevance: The values and qualities of Jesus' followers contribute to harmonious and compassionate relationships.

ch5- Social Teachings

13 let your light shine before others, that they may **see your good deeds** and glorify your Father in heaven....

20 For I tell you that **unless your righteousness surpasses** that of the Pharisees and the teachers of the law, you will certainly not enter the kingdom of heaven.

Relevance: Humanitarian acts should be done to glorify God rather than self.

ch5- Peace and Nonviolence

21-25 "You have heard that it was said to the people long ago, 'You shall not murder, and anyone who murders will be subject to judgment.' But I tell you that anyone who is **angry with a brother or sister** will be subject to judgment. Again, anyone who says to a brother or sister, **'Raca,'** is answerable to the court. And anyone who says, **'You fool!'** will be in danger of the fire of hell. "Therefore, if you are offering your gift at the altar and there remember that your brother or sister has something against you, leave your gift there in front of the altar. First go and be reconciled to them; then come and offer your gift. "**Settle matters quickly with your adversary who is taking you to court**. Do it while you are still together on the way, or your adversary may hand you over to the judge, and the judge may hand you over to the officer, and you may be thrown into prison.

Relevance: Avoiding anger and name-calling, is central to conflict resolution; seek peace in relationships and settle matters out of court to avoid maximum consequences.

ch5- Psychological Well-Being

27-28 "You have heard that it was said, 'You shall not commit adultery.' But I tell you that anyone who **looks at a woman lustfully has already committed adultery** with her in his heart.

Relevance: This is an important key sexual management principle to prevent sex addiction, prevalent today e.g. through internet pornography.

31-32 "It has been said, 'Anyone who divorces his wife must give her a certificate of divorce.' But I tell you that anyone who divorces his wife, except for sexual immorality, makes her the victim of adultery, and **anyone who marries a divorced woman commits adultery**.

Relevance: This principle supports family security and integrity especially important for healthy child development.

ch5- Social Teaching
33-37 But I tell you, **do not swear an oath** at all...All you need to say is simply 'Yes' or 'No'....

Relevance: Personal honesty is fundamental to basic trust essential to personal, professional, and business relationships in society.

ch5- Peace and Nonviolence
38-41 But I tell you, do not resist an evil person. If anyone slaps you on the right cheek, **turn to them the other cheek** also. And if anyone wants to sue you and take your shirt, hand over your coat as well. **If anyone forces** you to go one mile, go with them two miles.

43-45 You have heard that it was said, 'Love your neighbor and hate your enemy.' But I tell you, **love your enemies and pray for those who persecute you**, that you may be children of your Father in heaven.

Relevance: The teaching of nonviolence and nonretaliation in personal relationships is key to a harmonious family and community and central to resolving conflict.

ch6- Social Teaching
1-4 "Be careful not to practice your righteousness **in front of others to be seen by them**... But when you give to the needy, do not let your left hand know what your right hand is doing, so **that your giving may be in secret**.

Relevance: This concept promotes a selfless sincere motive in generosity, and in prayer vs.5-8, and in fasting vs.16-18.

9-13 This, then, is how you should pray: "...And **forgive us our debts, as we also have forgiven our debtors**...."

Relevance: This basic principle is the foundation of personal lending: forgive the debts of those who cannot pay you back.

ch6- Peace and Nonviolence
14-15 For **if you forgive other people when they sin against you, your heavenly Father will also forgive you**. But if you do not forgive others their sins, your Father will not forgive your sins.

Relevance: Forgiving others is highly valued.

ch6- Social Teaching
19-24 Do not store up for yourselves treasures on earth...But **store up for yourselves treasures in heaven**... No one can serve two masters. Either you will hate the one and love the other, or you will be devoted to the one and despise the other. You cannot serve both God and money.

Relevance: Value service to God by caring for the poor; build wealth for serving others rather than self.

ch6- Psychological Well-Being
25-34 ...**do not worry about your life**.... Therefore do not worry about tomorrow, for tomorrow will worry about itself. Each day has enough trouble of its own.

Relevance: A key remedy for anxiety is to live each day at a time; live in the present. Plan for tomorrow but don't worry about it.

ch7- Peace and Nonviolence
1-5 **Do not judge**, or you too will be judged. For in the same way you judge others, you will be judged, and with the measure you use, it will be measured to you. (John 8:7 He who is without sin among you, let him be the first to throw a stone at her [adulterous woman]).

Relevance: Judgment of others will result in judgment in return; be nonjudgmental and reduce conflict.

ch7- Social Teachings
7-12 **So in everything, do to others what you would have them do to you**, for this sums up the Law and the Prophets. (See also Luke 10:27 – **Love your neighbour as yourself**; Matthew 25:31-46 For I was hungry and you gave me food, I was thirsty and you gave me drink, I was a stranger and you welcomed me, I was naked and you clothed me, I was sick and you visited me, I was in prison and you came to me... **as you did it to one of the least of these my brothers, you did it to me**.)

Relevance: Reaching out to those in trouble is service to God.

ch7- Final Admonition
24 Therefore everyone who hears these **words of mine and puts them into practice** is like a wise man who built his house on the rock.

Relevance: Practicing what Jesus taught provides a solid foundation for wise living.

Meanings of the Cross

The suffering and death of Jesus of Nazareth on a Roman cross near Jerusalem, is the centre of Christian faith, and at the centre of the cross is the love of God. The meanings and implications of the cross are found throughout the earliest Christian writings:

The Power of God

For the message of the cross is foolishness to those who are perishing, but to us who are being saved it is the power of God.
– 1 Corinthians 1:18

Peace with God

….the *punishment* that brought us peace was on him.- Isaiah 53:5

"*He Himself bore our sins*" in His body on the tree, so that we might die to sin and live to righteousness. "By His stripes you are healed." For you were like sheep going astray, but now you have returned to the Shepherd and Overseer of your souls.
– 1 Peter 2:24,25

Righteousness in Reach

For our sake he *made him to be sin* who knew no sin, so that in him we might become the righteousness of God.

- 2 Corinthians 5:21

Forgiveness Given

Jesus said, "Father, forgive them, for they do not know what they are doing." - Luke 23:34

Forgive as the Lord forgave you. - Colossians 3:13

New Life Made Possible

How can we who died to sin live in it any longer? Or aren't you aware that all of us who were baptized into Christ Jesus were baptized into His death? We therefore were buried with Him through baptism into death, in order that, just as Christ was raised from the dead through the glory of the Father, we too may walk in newness of life. – Romans 6:2-4

Freedom from Sin

For we know that our old self was crucified with him so that the body ruled by sin might be done away with, that we should no longer be slaves to sin, for anyone who has died has been freed from sin. – Romans 6:6-7

Love Made Known

But God demonstrates his own love for us in this: While we were still sinners, Christ died for us.- Romans 5:8

And love consists in this: not that we loved God, but that He loved us and sent His Son as an atoning sacrifice for our sins. Beloved, if God so loved us, we also ought to love one another.
- 1 John 4:10-11

Nonviolence Exemplified

"Put your sword back in its place," Jesus said to him. "For all who draw the sword will die by the sword. Are you not aware that I can call on My Father, and He will at once put *at my disposal more than twelve legions of angels*?"- Matthew 26:52-53

Giving Defined

This is how we know what love is: Jesus *Christ laid down his life for us*. And we ought to lay down our lives for our brothers and sisters. If anyone has material possessions and sees a brother or sister in need but has no pity on them, how can the love of God be in that person? - 1 John 3:16-17

For you know the grace of our Lord Jesus Christ, that though he was rich, yet *for your sake he became poor*, so that you *through his poverty* might become rich. - 2 Corinthians 8:9

Endurance in Facing Suffering (even when you have done nothing wrong)

"Father, if you are willing, please take this cup of suffering away from me. Yet *I want your will to be done, not mine*." - Luke 22:42

....fixing our eyes on Jesus, the pioneer and perfecter of faith. For the joy set before him he *endured the cross*, scorning its shame, and sat down at the right hand of the throne of God.
- Hebrews 12:2

For to this you were called, because Christ also suffered for you, leaving you an example, that you should follow in His footsteps: "He committed no sin, and no deceit was found in His mouth." When they heaped abuse on Him, He did not retaliate; *when He suffered, He made no threats, but entrusted Himself to Him who judges justly.* - 1 Peter 2:21-23

HOW TO BECOME A CHRISTIAN

Practicing the Presence of God

Spiritual Mindfulness

Practicing the Presence of God

Spiritual Mindfulness

by Daniel Keeran, MSW

1 John 3:6
...and people who stay one in their hearts with him won't keep on sinning.
If they do keep on sinning, they don't know Christ, and they have never seen him
Contemporary English Version (CEV)

"Where is God? I don't see any God. Show me God, and I will believe."

How many times have you heard this? And maybe you are hearing it more as time goes by. We all have friends or family members who doubt that God exists, and sometimes you may have doubts about God's presence or sometimes you may feel very distant from God or may simply not be aware of his presence.

Peter says our confidence is not about seeing Him but about loving and believing in Him.

1 Peter 1:7-9 "**Though you have not seen him, you love him; and even though you do not see him now, you believe in him** and are filled with an inexpressible and glorious joy, for you are receiving the goal of your faith, the salvation of your souls."

The difference between a secular mindset and a sacred mindset is that in the secular life, one engages in daily life disconnected and without awareness of God. In the sacred life, one engages in daily life with a strong awareness of God. In the sacred life, the child of God sees everything and every moment in the context of the spiritual and says, "The God of the universe who holds everything together is fully and personally present right here, right now."

When you read sacred scripture, you are struck in every verse by the writers' **constant awareness of God**. This is in stark contrast with the **secular life** in which one merely seeks the good life in harmony with one's neighbour but without any awareness of God. When a child is very young she is aware of God, then from pre-school to university, the secular worldview is taught, and the secular media and the secular workplace prohibit God, or place faith in a negative light. So the faith community is an oasis where we fill up on God. Then we leave the community, the secular chains go back on, and God is left behind. Is that what happens?

To live spiritually and to break off the secular chains, **believe God is always present, always caring, always guiding and directing and nurturing, always eager to hear from you, always forgiving, always loving, always reaching out to you, always watching and waiting for you to turn to him, and when you do turn to God, he sings and rejoices over you. Do you believe it?**

If you believe it, you can know it, then **you can see God at work everywhere** and hear God's constant reassurance and encouragement.

Psalm 139:7-10 "Where can I go from your Spirit? Where can I flee from your presence? If I go up to the heavens, **you are there**; if I make my bed in the depths, you are there. If I rise on the wings of the dawn, if I settle on the far side of the sea, even there your hand will guide me, your right hand will hold me fast."

God is present and near to you right here, right now. What emotions do you feel? If you believe it you can see and feel God with your heart right now.

God loves you and He is so proud of you

Zephaniah 3:17 "The LORD your God is with you, he is mighty to save. He will **take great delight in you, he will quiet you with his love, he will rejoice over you with singing**."

Listen to God singing and rejoicing over you. What do you feel? Maybe you feel so loved, so accepted, so cared for by the Creator of the universe that you think for a moment **it could last forever, and that is exactly what God wants for you**.

Psalm 147:11 "The **LORD delights** in those who fear him, who put their hope in his unfailing love."

Believe the Lord is proud of you. What do you feel? Yes, God is proud of you. Maybe you feel peaceful and happy, a sense of deep contentment. This picture of delight the Father feels about you is described in the story of the prodigal son.

Luke 15:20-23 "So he got up and went to his father. But while he was still a long way off, his father saw him and was **filled with compassion** for him; he ran to his son, **threw his arms around him and kissed him**. The son said to him, 'Father, I have sinned against heaven and against you. I am no longer worthy to be called your son.' But the father said to his servants, 'Quick! Bring the best robe and put it on him. Put a ring on his finger and sandals on his feet. Bring the fattened calf and kill it. **Let's have a feast and celebrate**. For this son of mine was dead and is alive again; he was lost and is found.' So they began to celebrate."

If you believe God delights in you, loves you, and rejoices in song over you, then **you can see and hear God with the eyes and ears of your heart**. Can you begin to see and hear God and **sense his constant presence and love for you**?

Suppose God told someone to write a note and give it to you and the note said, "You can't see me, but I am very close to you right now and I want you to know that I love and care about you and that I am working in your life to make good things happen." How would you feel if you received that note? Wouldn't it be wonderful? Wouldn't you feel special and confident and have such peace that would never fade away? God has written such a note. It's called the Bible...the holy scriptures. It's a bit longer than a note.

Psalm 119:64 "The **earth is filled with your love, O LORD**; teach me your decrees." If you believe, you can know, and then you can see the evidence of God's love everywhere. Look around the room. See those in whom the Spirit lives. See all the gifts of God around you.

2 Corinthians 5:16 "So from now on we **regard no one from a worldly point of view**. Though we once regarded Christ in this way, we do so no longer."

God works directly in your life

to make everything work for your good and for his purposes.

Psalm 138:8 "The **LORD will fulfill his purpose** for me; your love, O LORD, endures forever...." God is making things happen in your life to serve his purposes. You do believe God will fulfill his purpose for you. You do feel his constant enduring love for you.

Psalm 145:20 "The **LORD watches** over all who love him..." You do believe God watches over you. **God is looking at you right now, right here**. Do you know it? What emotion comes up inside you right now as you sense God's attention focused on you? Does it make you want to smile?

Romans 8:28 "And we know that **all things work together** for good to them that love God, to them who are the **called according to his purpose**." You have the confidence that God is working in your life and will make everything work out even through suffering and tragedy. Look for ways God is working in your life and give thanks in everything, knowing God is working in all things for your good.

Proverbs 16:9 "In his heart a man plans his course, but **the LORD determines his steps**."

Ephesians 5:20 "always **giving thanks to God the Father for everything**, in the name of our Lord Jesus Christ."

Remember the words of Job: "The Lord gives and the Lord takes away. Blessed is the name of the Lord." And "Even if the Lord slays me, yet will I serve him." You can have the faith of Job. You can feel those chains of doubt and unbelief falling away.

God will always love you and nothing will ever change that. **You are surrounded by his love and that will never change.**

God's own love has been poured into our hearts.

Romans 5:5 "God has **poured out his love** into our hearts by the Holy Spirit, whom he has given us."

If you believe God's love is in you, then you can love everyone as God loves. Remember that God loves the world so much that he gave Jesus to suffer and die and take away the sins of the world. What a wonderful gift to have inside you! God's own love.

Romans 8:35-39 "**Who shall separate us from the love of Christ**? Shall trouble or hardship or persecution or famine or nakedness or danger or sword? As it is written: 'For your sake we face death all day long; we are considered as sheep to be slaughtered.' No, in all these things we are more than conquerors through him who loved us. For I am convinced that neither death nor life, neither angels nor demons, neither the present nor the future, nor any powers, neither height nor depth, nor anything else in all creation, will be able to separate us from the love of God that is in Christ Jesus our Lord."

Faith is how we enter into eternal reality; how we come to God

Today I want you to be aware of God's presence and nearness. God is Spirit, so you cannot see Him with your physical eyes, but you can see God with the eyes of your heart, the eyes of faith. You can believe and know that God is near you and in you. Then knowing this, you can look at God and see God looking back at you. You can speak to God and hear God speaking to you. **God is always speaking and saying more than you can hear.** Your mind and heart cannot possibly contain or hear all that God is saying. Can your mind contain all that is written? His word is living and active. Your heart must be selective because if you heard all that God is saying to you, you would be overwhelmed. **The more of God's word you know, the more you will be able to hear what God is saying to you personally.**

2 Corinthians 4:18 "So we **fix our eyes not on what is seen, but on what is unseen**. For what is seen is temporary, but what is unseen is eternal."

Things that are seen are temporary but things unseen are eternal. So through every word of God, that Jesus says we live by, we know about God and about his relationship with us. So when we read or hear God's word, we believe it, and **by this we know God, see God, and hear God, not with physical eyes and ears but by the eyes and ears of our hearts, the eyes and ears of faith**.

Jesus made this direct reference when he said, "Having **eyes they see not and ears they hear not**"....he's talking about having the eyes and ears of faith.

Being aware of God requires engaging in certain kinds of activity that encourage faith. Our physical eyes see material things, and so God is often not in our minds. The saying "out of sight out of mind" is true. Because we do not see God with our physical eyes, God is not in our mind. Yet **God is always present, and so we must encourage one another to be aware of God's presence by talking about spiritual things and listening to spiritual teaching, singing praises and spiritual songs, and reading God's word.**

We are made alive

Since we walk around and breathe in these bodies, we naturally think we are alive. The following words must be taken to mean we are made alive (with Christ) in a spiritual way and forgiven of sins, and this is associated with the act of baptism (overwhelmed with physical water) when it is done as a conscious act of faith:

Colossians 2:12-13 "….having been buried with him in baptism, in which you were also raised with him through your faith in the working of God, who raised him from the dead. When you were dead in your sins and in the uncircumcision of your flesh, God made you alive with Christ. He forgave us all our sins…."

Identical terms are used in Ephesians 2:4-6, but without a direct mention of baptism:

"But because of his great love for us, God, who is rich in mercy, made us alive with Christ even when we were dead in transgressions—it is by grace you have been saved. And God raised us up with Christ…."

Why doesn't God just show himself, or work a miracle, or shout with a booming voice from the sky?

1 Corinthians 1:22-24 "**Jews demand miraculous signs and Greeks look for wisdom**, but we preach Christ crucified: a stumbling block to Jews and foolishness to Gentiles, but to those whom God has called, both Jews and Greeks, Christ the power of God and the wisdom of God."

Hebrews 11:6 "And **without faith it is impossible to please God**, because anyone who comes to him must believe that he exists and that he rewards those who earnestly seek him."

"The just shall **live by faith**" Romans 1:17, and by this faith we know God, we know his presence, we know his love. If God's word says it, then we know it is real even if we do not see with our physical eyes.

Faith says: James 4:8 "Come near to God and **he will come near** to you." Believe and know that God is near you right now. What emotions are you feeling? Maybe a little anxious but also loved and assured.

Faith says: Hebrews 10:22 "let us **draw near to God with a sincere heart in full assurance of faith**..."

Faith says: 1 John 4:12 "No one has ever seen God; but if we love one another, **God lives in us** and his love is made complete in us."

Faith says: Acts 17:27-28 "...reach out for him and find him, though **he is not far** from each one of us. 'For **in him we live** and move and have our being.' As some of your own poets have said, 'We are his offspring.' " Your life depends upon God. God gave us the spirit of life in each of us, and he is near you right now. Know and feel the presence of God right now.

Faith says: John 14:23 Jesus replied, "If anyone loves me, he will obey my teaching. My Father will love him, and **we will come to him and make our home with him**." You follow his teaching. You are living in the center of his will and trusting his grace. Then you know God is with you right now, and when you sleep, when you go about your daily activities, in every moment God is present and living with you and in you because **"your body is a temple of the Holy Spirit, who is in you, whom you have received from God"** 1 Corinthians 6:19.

Faith says: 2 Cor.1:3-7 "Praise be to the God and Father of our Lord Jesus Christ, the **Father of compassion and the God of all comfort, who comforts us in all our troubles**, so that we can comfort those in any trouble with the comfort we ourselves have received from God. For just as the sufferings of Christ flow over into our lives, so also through Christ our comfort overflows."

Believe God cares about you so much that he is here right now to comfort you, to reassure you, to let you know that he is working everything out for your good. He is the God of all comfort for every kind of trouble.

Faith says: Psalm 23:4 "Even though I walk through the valley of the shadow of death, I will fear no evil, **for you are with me**; your rod and your staff, they comfort me."

Do you know Christ?

Paul says in Philippians 3:10 **I want to know Christ** and the power of His resurrection and the fellowship of His sufferings, being conformed to Him in His death, so that I may somehow attain to the resurrection from the dead.

In Hebrews 1:1-3 we find these wonderful words: After God spoke long ago in various portions and in various ways to our ancestors through the prophets, in these last days **he has spoken to us in a son, whom he appointed heir of all things, and through whom he created the world**. The Son is the radiance of his glory and the representation of his essence, and he sustains all things by his powerful word, and so when he had accomplished cleansing for sins, he sat down at the right hand of the Majesty on high.

The Spirit of God can live within

In order to have the Spirit of God living within, one must live according to or bear the fruits of the Spirit.

Romans 8:5-11 Those who live according to the flesh have their minds set on what the flesh desires; but **those who live in accordance with the Spirit have their minds set on what the Spirit desires**. The mind governed by the flesh is death, but the mind governed by the Spirit is life and peace. The mind governed by the flesh is hostile to God; it does not submit to God's law, nor can it do so. Those who are in the realm of the flesh cannot please God. You, however, are not in the realm of the flesh but are in the realm of the Spirit, if indeed **the Spirit of God lives in you**. And if anyone does not have the Spirit of Christ, they do not belong to Christ. But if Christ is in you, then even though your body is subject to death because of sin, the Spirit gives life because of righteousness. And if **the Spirit of him who raised Jesus from the dead is living in you**, he who raised Christ from the dead will also give life to your mortal bodies because of his Spirit who lives in you.

Galatians 5:22-25 But **the fruit of the Spirit is love, joy, peace, forbearance, kindness, goodness, faithfulness, gentleness and self-control**. Against such things there is no law. **Those who belong to Christ Jesus have crucified the flesh with its passions and desires**. Since we live by the Spirit, let us keep in step with the Spirit.

Have you seen Jesus our Lord?

Matthew 25:39-41 'When did we see you sick or in prison and go to visit you?' He will reply, 'I tell you the truth, **whatever you did for one of the least of these brothers of mine, you did for me.**'

I like this fictional version of the 4th wise man. The story is that there was a 4th wise man but he became ill and could not go with the other three to see the baby Jesus and to lay their gifts at his feet. So they left without him. Then when he was feeling better the wise man started out to take his precious jewel as a gift for the new Saviour King of Israel. But on his way, he met a poor dying beggar, so he sold the jewel to buy the beggar some food shelter and clothing, then came a leper, then a man robbed and left for dead, and after many years he had spent all he had on caring for those in need. Many years later, he was in Jerusalem and heard that Jesus was condemned to be crucified. The wise man hurried to see Jesus carrying his cross. Jesus looked at the wise man and smiled.

When you see the homeless or anyone in trouble, draw near to them, attend to them, and then you will draw near to Jesus. **Don't walk by on the other side.**

Who is this God?

John 1:3 "**Through him all things were made**; without him nothing was made that has been made." The universe from the smallest atom or single-cell organism to the vastness of space and billions of galaxies...He made it all.

Colossians 1:17 "He is before all things, and **in him all things hold together**."

When you think about God being present, **think about who God is. Then think about his promise to be near you and words of faith that this God is really present in you and with you.**

This almighty **all-powerful creator God who holds everything together is sitting right next to you right now. Look at him with the eyes of your heart.**

Then listen with the ears of faith. God is always speaking to you more than you can possibly hear.

What is God saying?

I love you more than you can imagine. I care about you. I know you better than you know yourself, and I will always give you what you need. I love you so much that I suffered and died and took all your sins and punishment upon myself. I forgive you. I forgave you when you were immersed into Jesus for the forgiveness of your sins as my servant Peter spoke in Acts 2:38.

Psalm 139:1-4 "O LORD, you have searched me and you know me. You know when I sit and when I rise; **you perceive my thoughts from afar**. You discern my going out and my lying down; **you are familiar with all my ways. Before a word is on**

my tongue you know it completely, O LORD." God knows you personally and intimately. He knows you far better than you know yourself.

Matthew 10:30 "And even the very **hairs of your head are all numbered**." Does anyone here know how many hairs are on your head? That's just a tiny example of **how thoroughly God knows you**.

Matthew 6:8 "...for your **Father knows what you need** before you ask him." You don't have to worry about what you need. God already knows what you need and what is best for you.

God says, I will make good things happen from suffering. I will comfort and guide you when you trust me.

Proverbs 3:5-6 "Trust in the LORD with all your heart; and lean not on your own understanding. In all your ways acknowledge him, and **he will direct your paths**."

God says, ask me for anything and I will do it when you want to serve my purpose. When we ask God for something, we need to humbly say, "Lord I ask this only if it serves your purpose and gives you glory, because otherwise I don't want it."

God says, when you ask for my forgiveness, you know that I will forgive you and will not be angry with you.

God is eager to hear from you.

God is eagerly waiting for your conversation. Talk to him now and often.

"I love you Lord, and I give my life to serve and worship you. Thank you for always being here for me. Thank you for my life, and for my health. I depend on you for everything. Help me to always remember to talk to you and to serve you. Give me wisdom to do great things for you my Lord. Open doors for me.

Make things happen and give me opportunities to share your love and forgiveness with the lost and hurting around me."

Psalm 42:8 "By day **the LORD directs his love**, at night his song is with me— a prayer to the God of my life." Remember God's love directed toward you today.

1 Peter 3:12 "For the **eyes of the Lord** are on the righteous and **his ears are attentive** to their prayer..." Remember God is present, watching and waiting for you to speak to him.

James 4:2 "**You do not have, because you do not ask God**." He is ready to answer your prayer.

1 John 5:14 "This is the **confidence we have in approaching God**: that **if we ask anything according to his will, he hears us**. And if we know that he hears us—whatever we ask—we know that we have what we asked of him."

God says we can go to him with confidence that **he will answer when we ask anything to serve his purpose**.

James 1:5-7" If any of you **lacks wisdom, he should ask God**, who **gives generously to all** without finding fault, and it will be given to him. But when he asks, he must believe and not doubt, because he who doubts is like a wave of the sea, blown and tossed by the wind. That man should not think he will receive anything from the Lord."

Are you confused about what to do? Ask the Lord for wisdom, and know that you will receive it.

Psalm 16:7 "I will praise **the LORD, who counsels me**; even at night my heart instructs me." When you lie awake at night, listen for counsel from the Lord.

Spiritual Practice

Here is an example of what you can say to come near to God in faith.

First, remind yourself:

"God made the universe and holds everything together. Jesus promised to make his home with me. God is always near and present because I live and move in God who is all around me. This God is here now, near me and seeing me, and eager to hear from me. Now in faith believing and knowing God is as close as my breath, I can hear his voice loving and forgiving me. I know that I can tell him what I feel and what I want to do, and he will do it if it will serve his purpose and glorify him because that's all I ever want to do."

Then think something like:

"Thank you, God. I know you are here right now. God, use me up. Show me things that will encourage others and serve your purpose. Thank you for always being with me to guide me and make good things happen. I will always trust and never doubt you, Lord. But if I do doubt, I know you will still be there patiently and eagerly waiting for me. In Jesus' precious name. Amen."

HOW TO BECOME A CHRISTIAN

This free download book has been used effectively in personal evangelism. This link gives a formatted booklet to be printed https://www.box.com/s/79a0f4p8xt5fmrydws8a This link gives the pages in consecutive order for internet or email use https://www.box.com/lovegod